Preface

The Rhythm Drill Book Complete Second Edition

The Rhythm Drill Book Complete Second Edition is an excellent resource for improving recognition of rhythmic patterns and metric pulse. This updated volume has been reorganized and augmented with more exercises in a greater variety of meters to better serve aspiring musicians. Through regular practice, these drills will help to develop a strong sense of rhythm and at the same time improve sight reading abilities.

The Rhythm Drill Book is divided into three chapters, each of these chapters is also available as a separate volume:

- Junior — RCM* Preparatory to Level 4
- Intermediate — RCM Levels 5 to 8
- Senior — RCM Levels 9 to ARCT

The following notes and abbreviations apply throughout series. Patterns and meters loosely follow those found in the graded RCM* 2015 Syllabus. In the event a figure or time signature is not present in the *Drill Book*, blank measures are provided at the end of each chapter to write customized examples. Ties and "pick-ups" have not been used but they can be added as required. White boxes indicate the first time a rhythm or meter is featured. In the *Rhythm Index* at the beginning of each chapter . . .

p.	= the page on which a specific rhythm is featured,
v.v.	= "vice versa", rhythms that are found in reverse,
vs.	= "verses", triple against duple patterns.

For short video introductions to *The Rhythm Drill Book* and other publications in the Piano Workbook Series, visit pianoworkbook.com.

Table of Contents

Junior Level

Rhythm Index

	$\frac{4}{4}$	$\frac{3}{4}$	$\frac{2}{4}$	$\frac{5}{4}$
♩ , 𝅗𝅥	p. 8	p. 11	p. 15	/
𝅗𝅥.	p. 9	p. 11	/	/
𝅝	p. 9	/	/	/
♫	p. 12	p. 13	p. 15	/
𝄽	p. 16	p. 17	p. 20	/
♬	p. 18	p. 19	p. 20	/
♩. ♪	p. 24	p. 25	p. 30	/
♩. ♫	p. 28	p. 29	p. 30	/
♩ ♫	p. 34	p. 35	p. 38	/
♫ ♩	p. 36	p. 37	p. 39	/
♫ ♫ V.V.	/	/	/	p. 51
𝅗𝅥. 𝅗𝅥 V.V.	/	/	/	p. 51

Rhythm Index

Rhythm	3/8	6/8	5/8	7/8
	p. 42	p. 46	/	/
	p. 42	/	/	/
	p. 43	/	/	/
	p. 43	/	/	/
V.V.	p. 44	p. 47	/	/
	/	p. 46	/	/
	p. 44	/	/	/
	p. 45	/	/	/
	p. 45	/	/	/
V.V.	/	/	p. 50	p. 52
V.V.	/	/	p. 50	p. 52

Preparatory

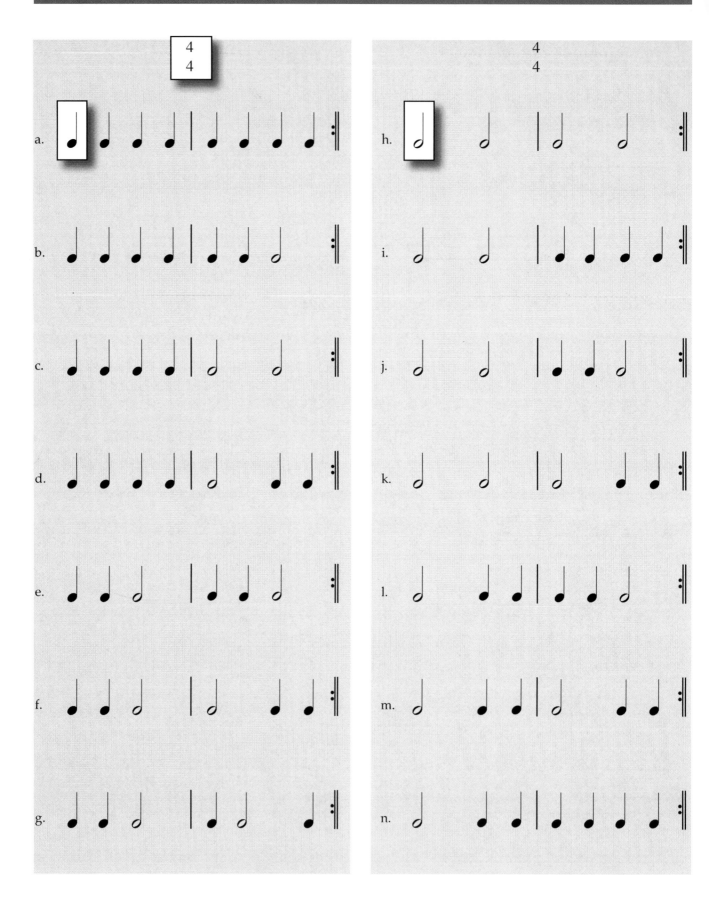

© 2018 Barbara M. Siemens PW-R2J

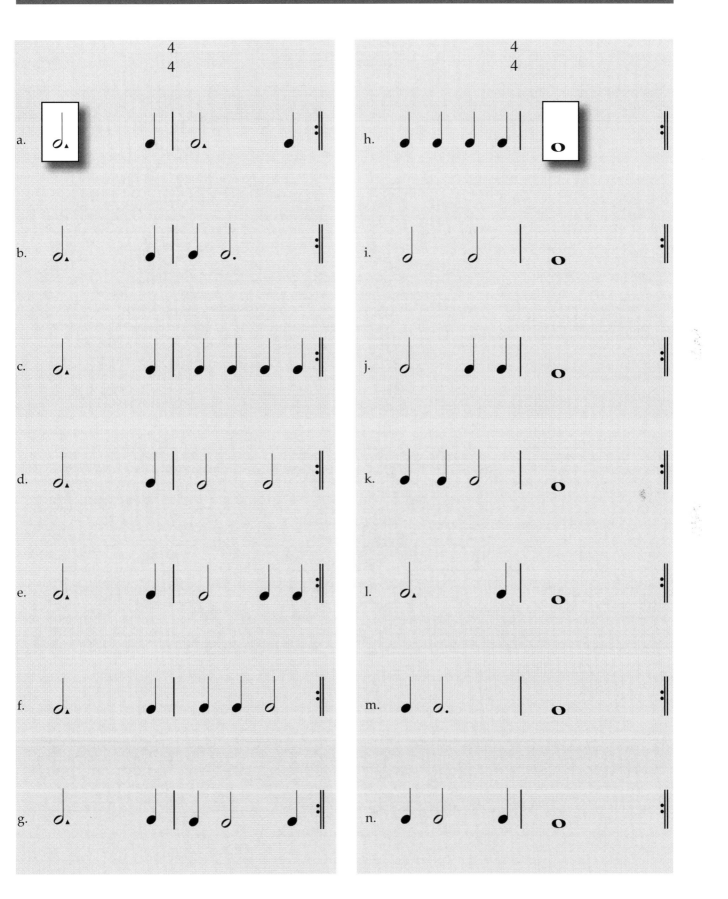

9

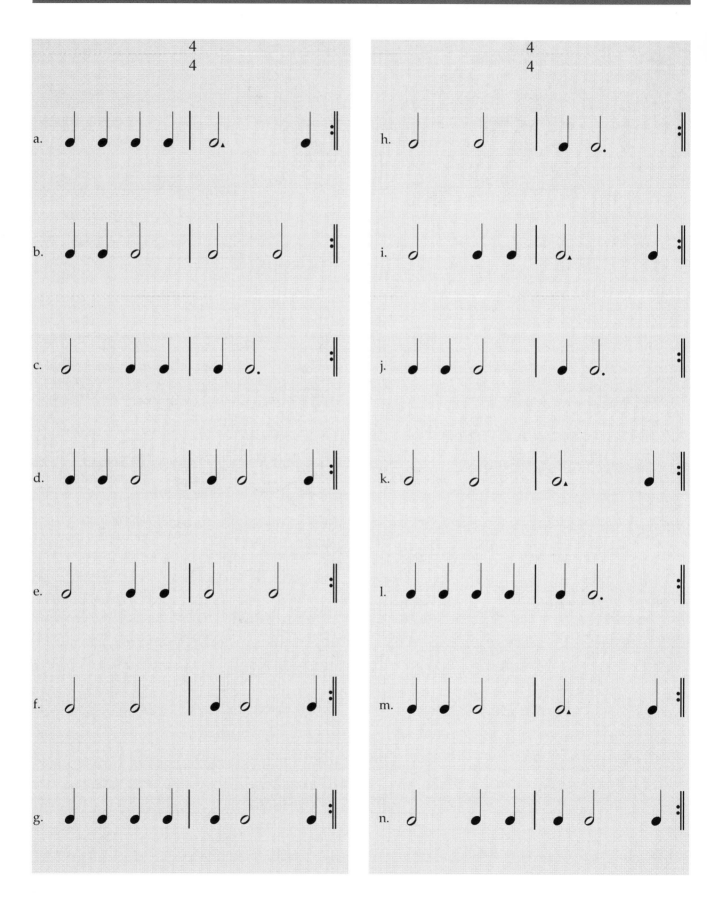

© 2018 Barbara M. Siemens   PW-R2J

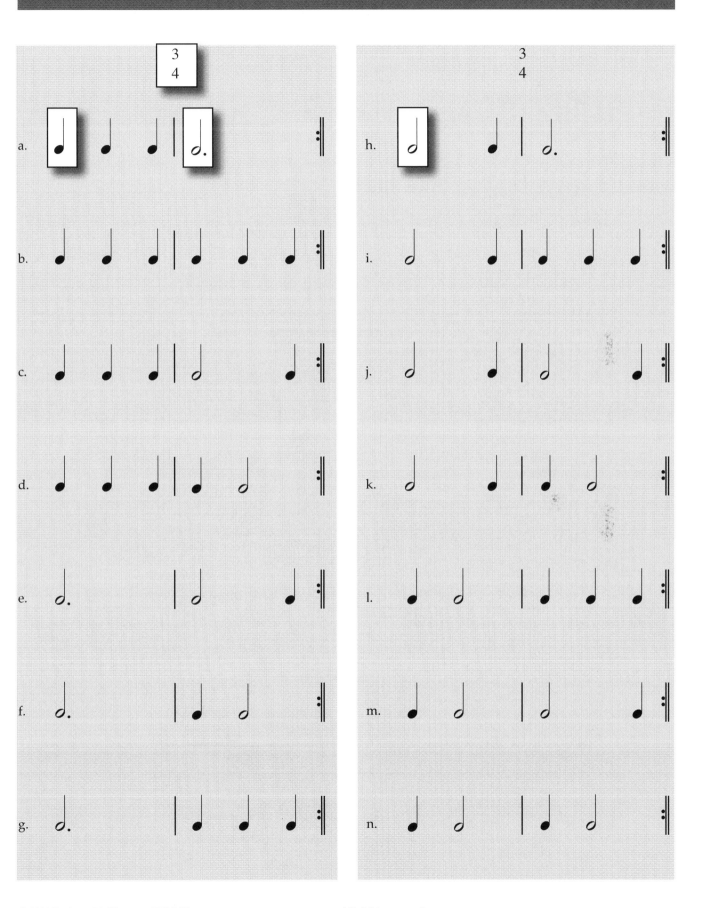

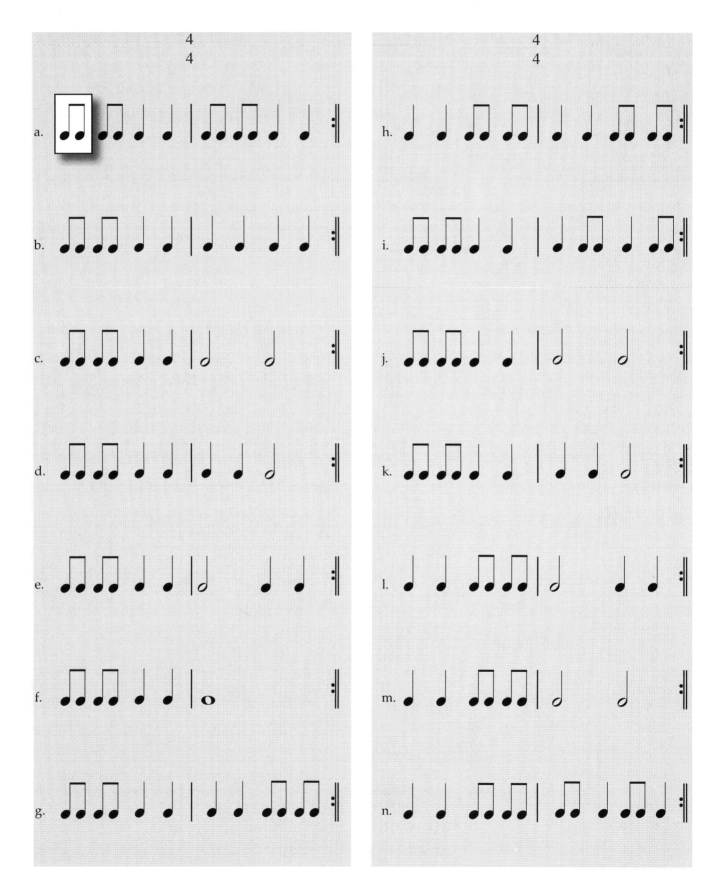

© 2018 Barbara M. Siemens PW-R2J

Preparatory

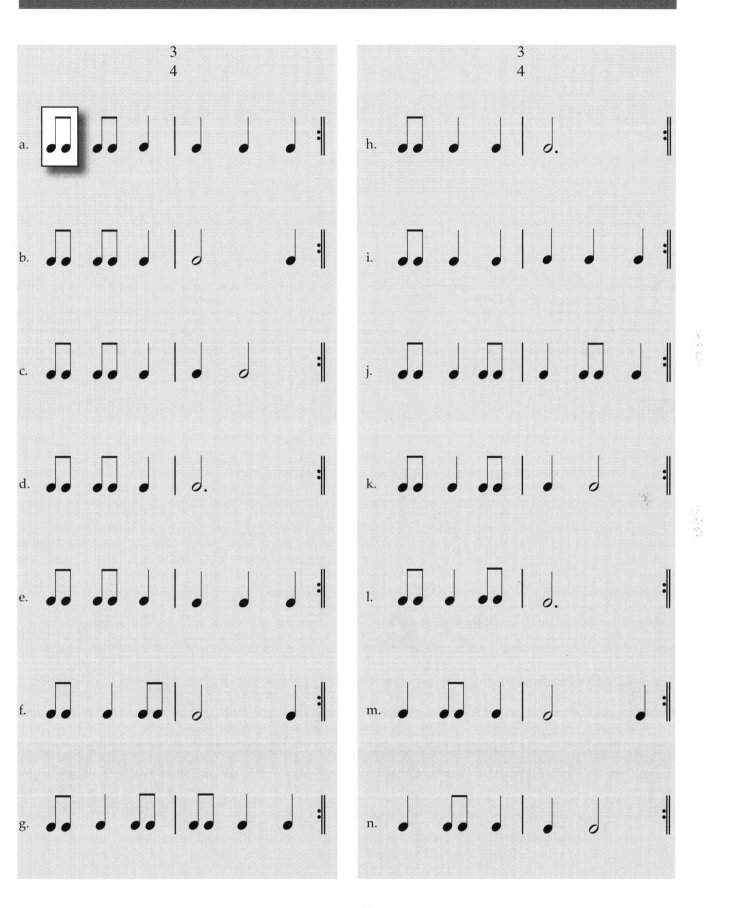

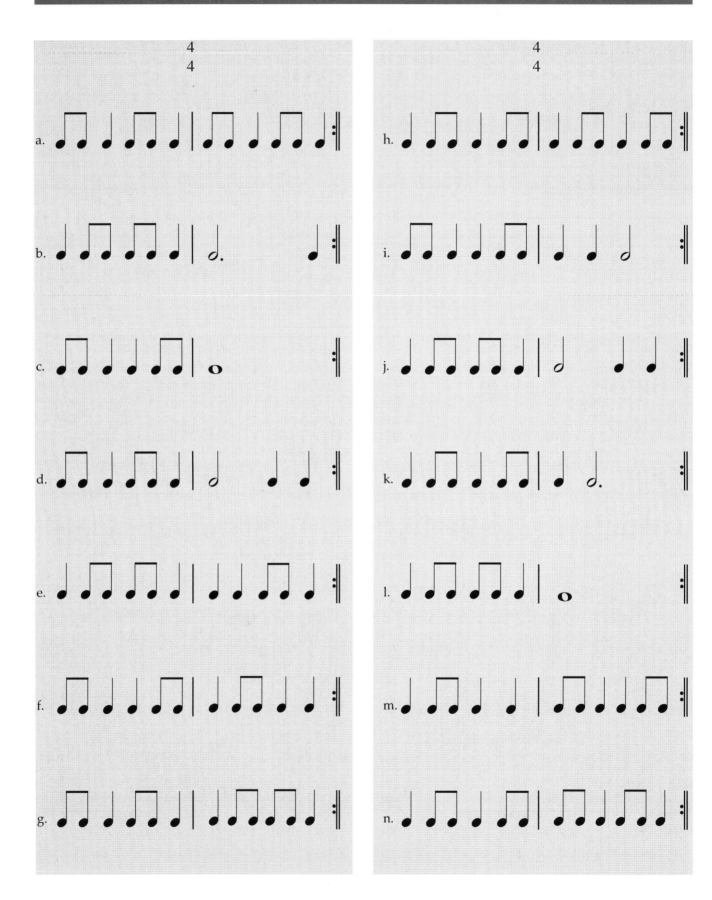

© 2018 Barbara M. Siemens   PW-R2J

Preparatory

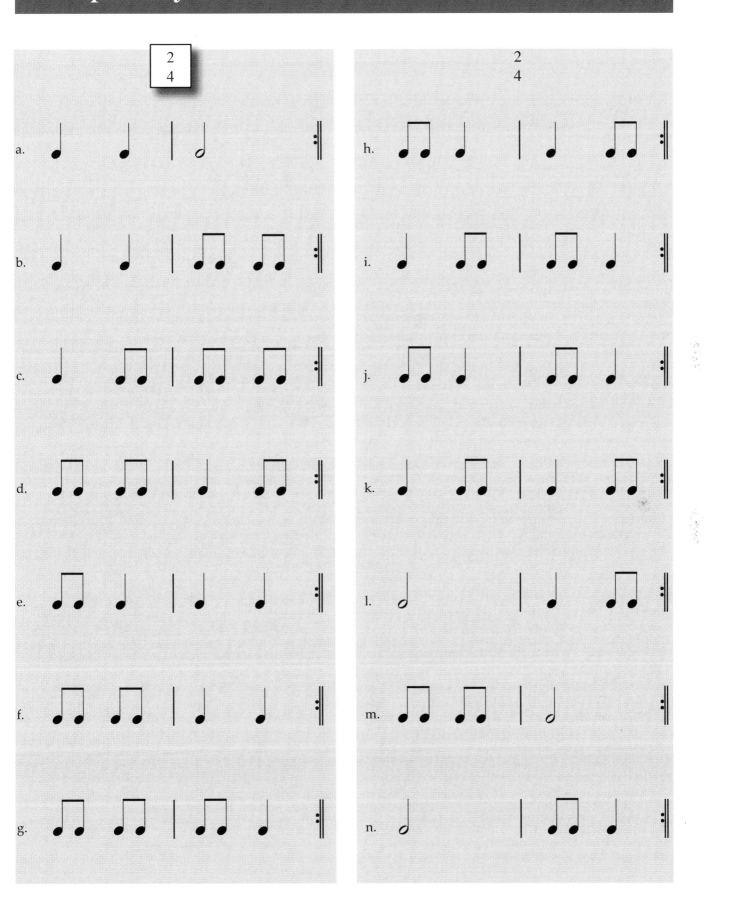

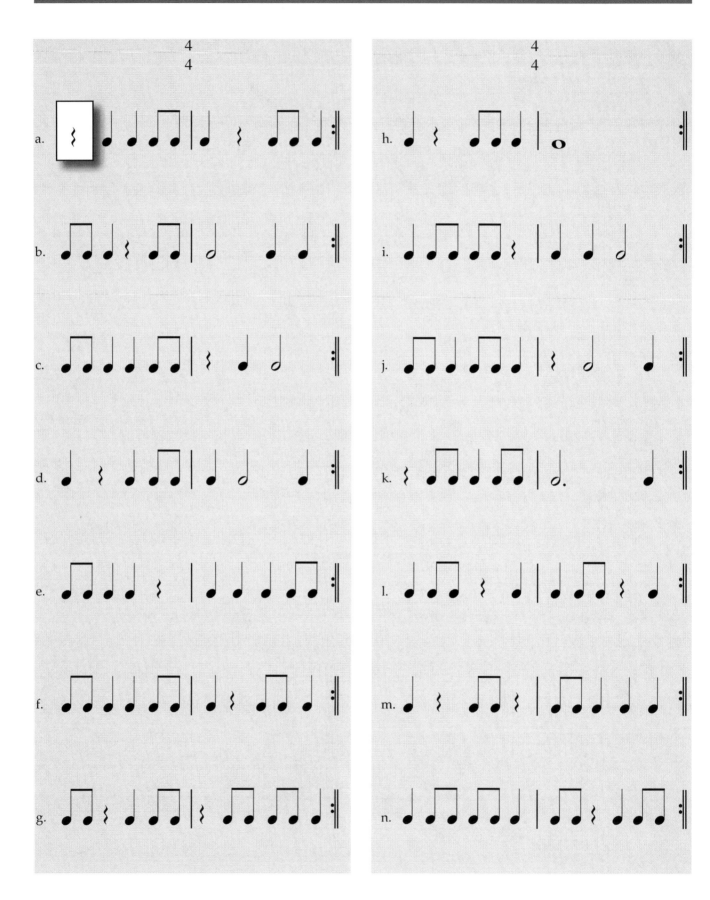

© 2018 Barbara M. Siemens PW-R2J

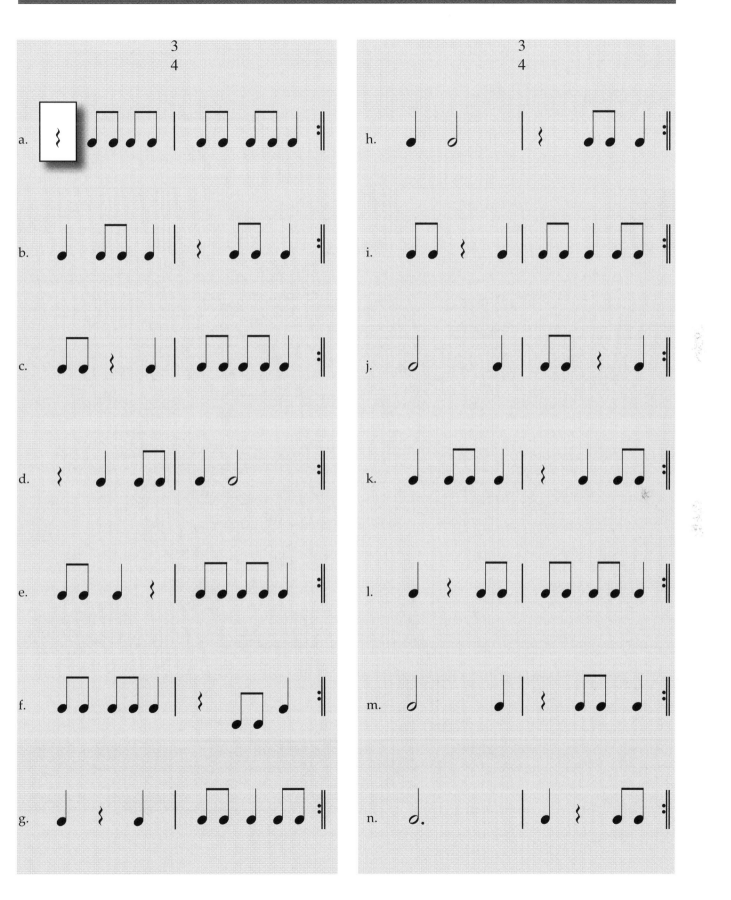

All rights reserved.

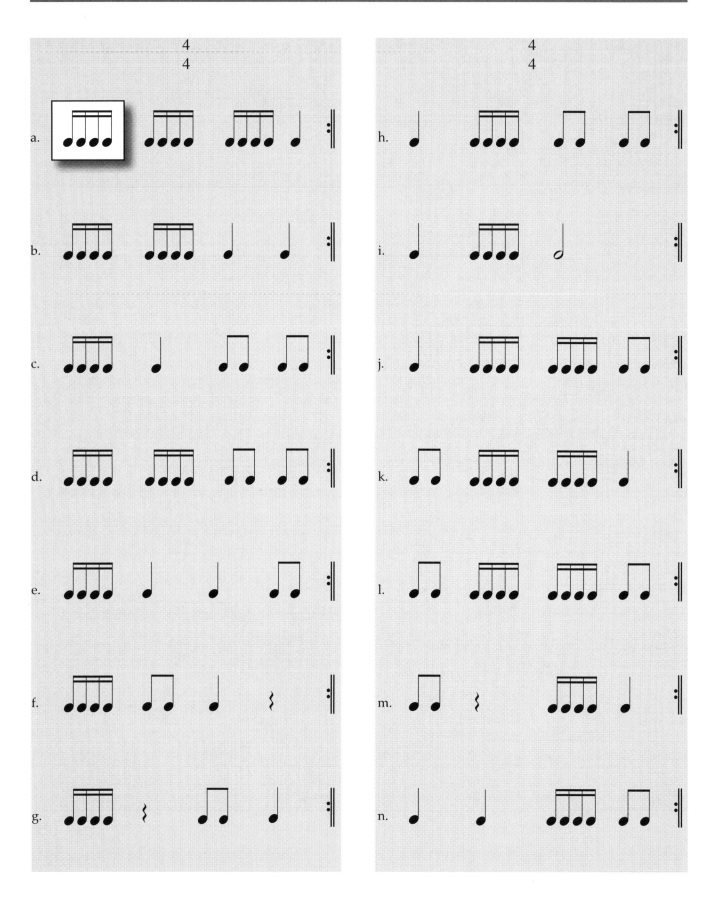

© 2018 Barbara M. Siemens   PW-R2J

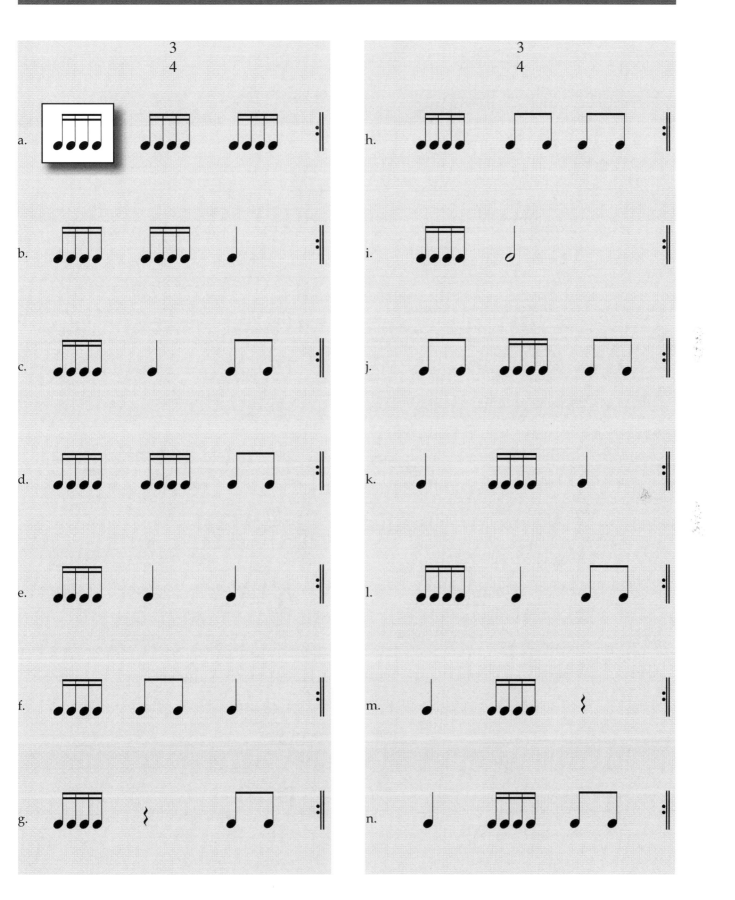

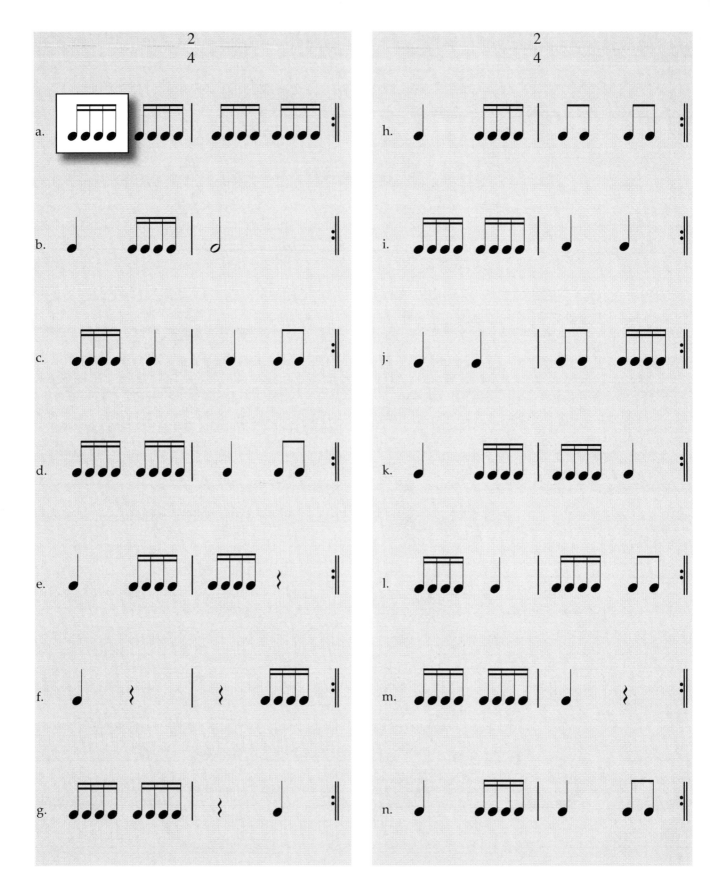

© 2018 Barbara M. Siemens PW-R2J

Junior

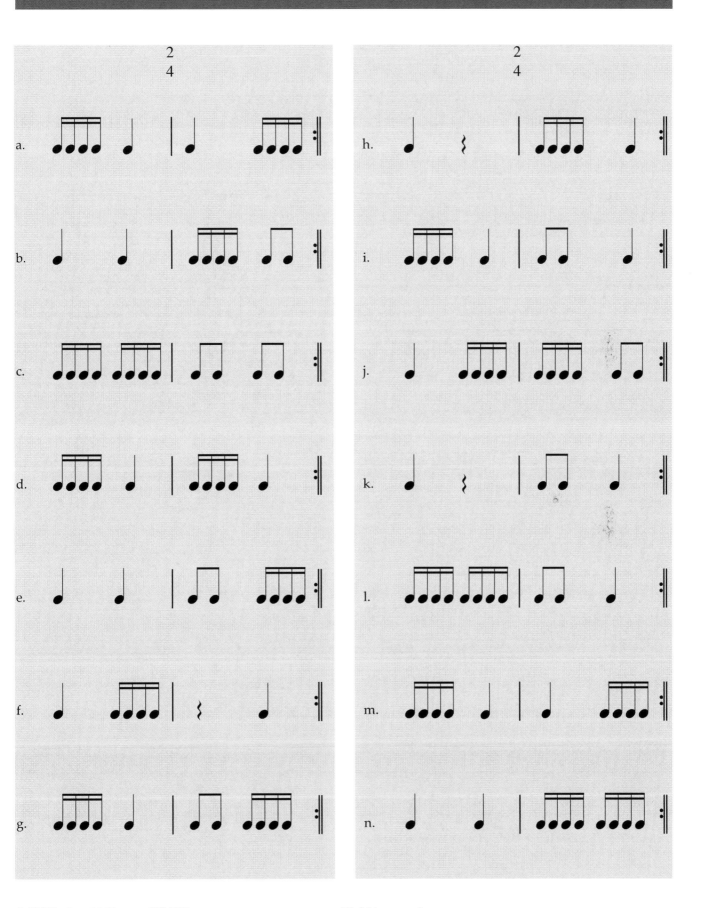

Junior

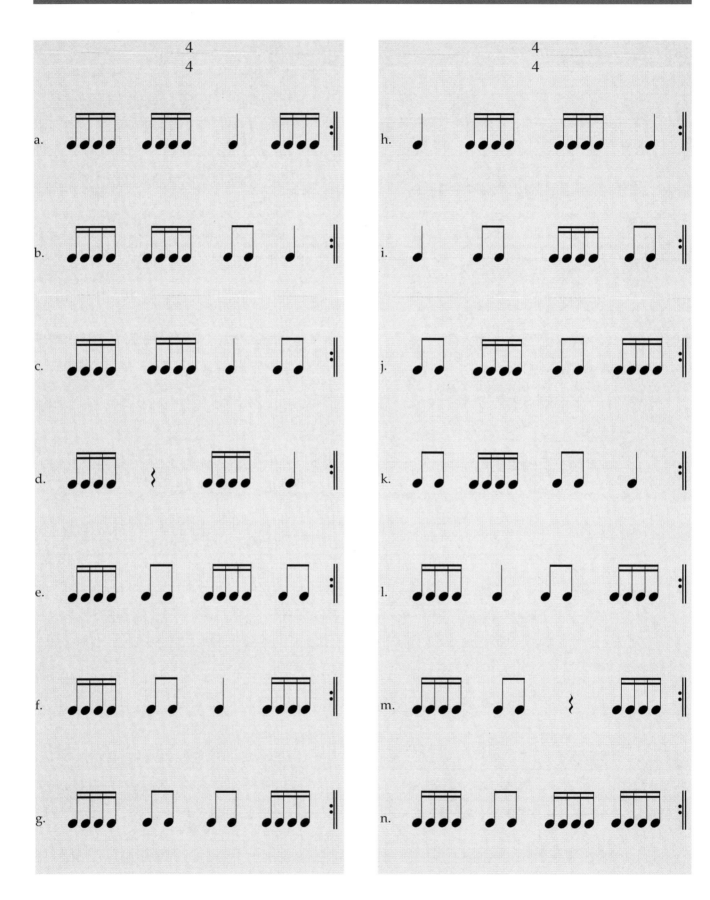

© 2018 Barbara M. Siemens   PW-R2J

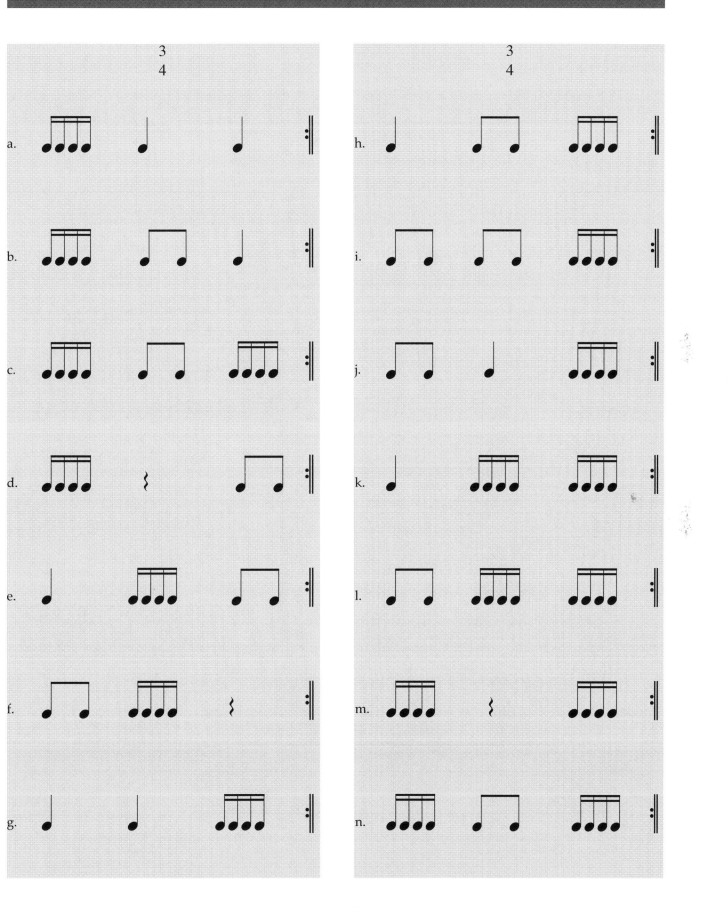

© 2018 Barbara M. Siemens   PW-R2J

23

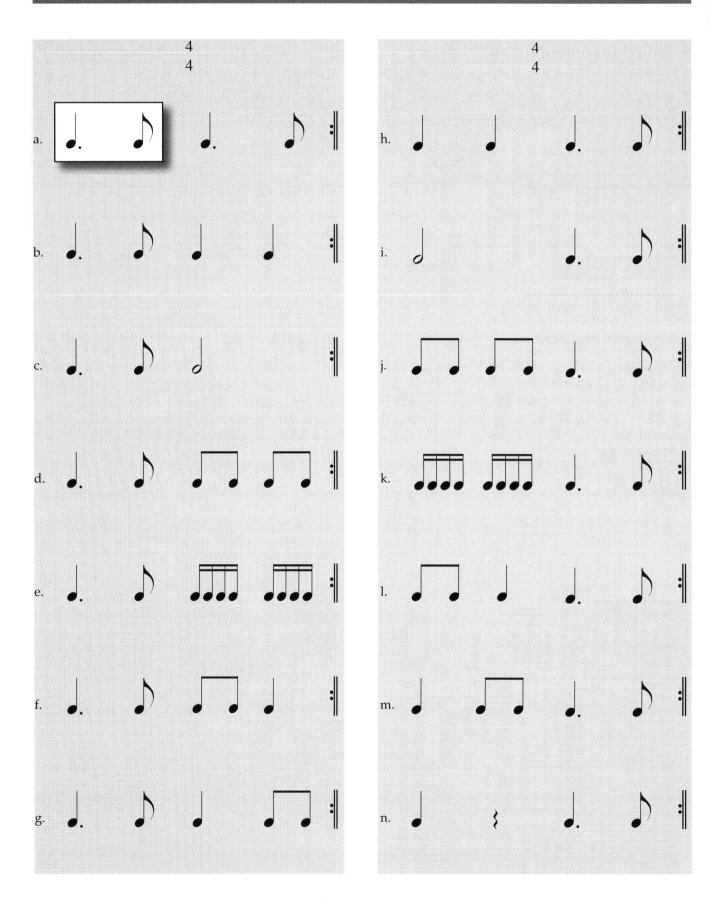

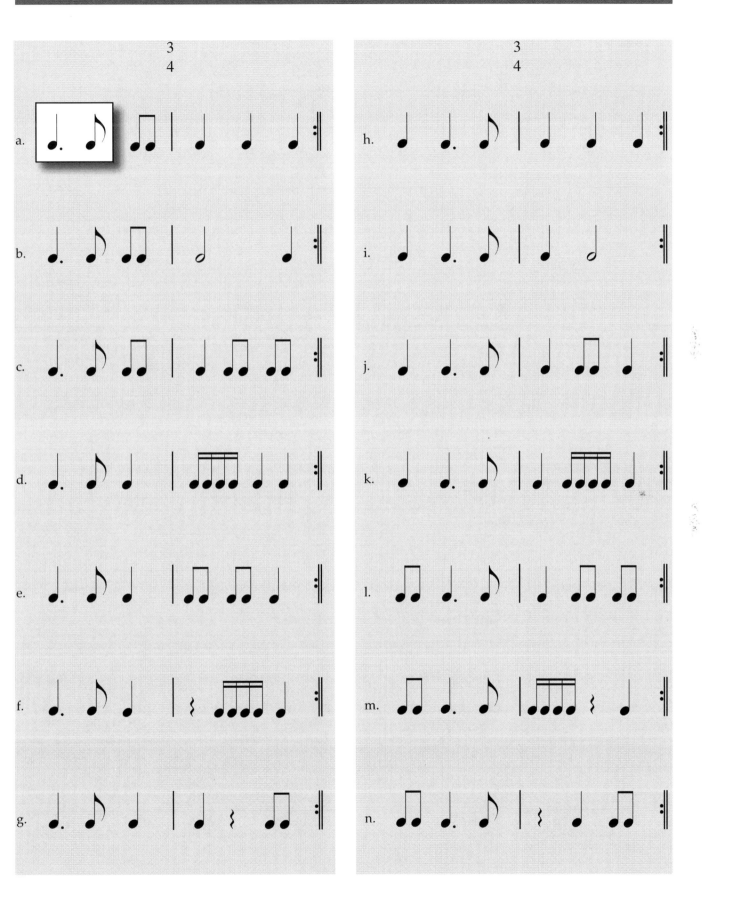

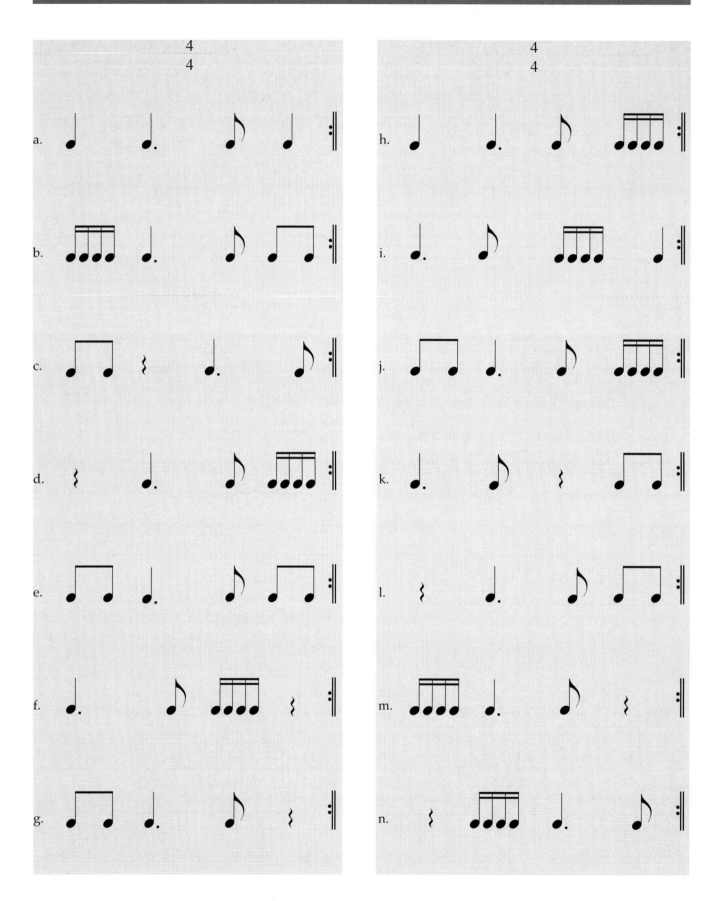

© 2018 Barbara M. Siemens PW-R2J

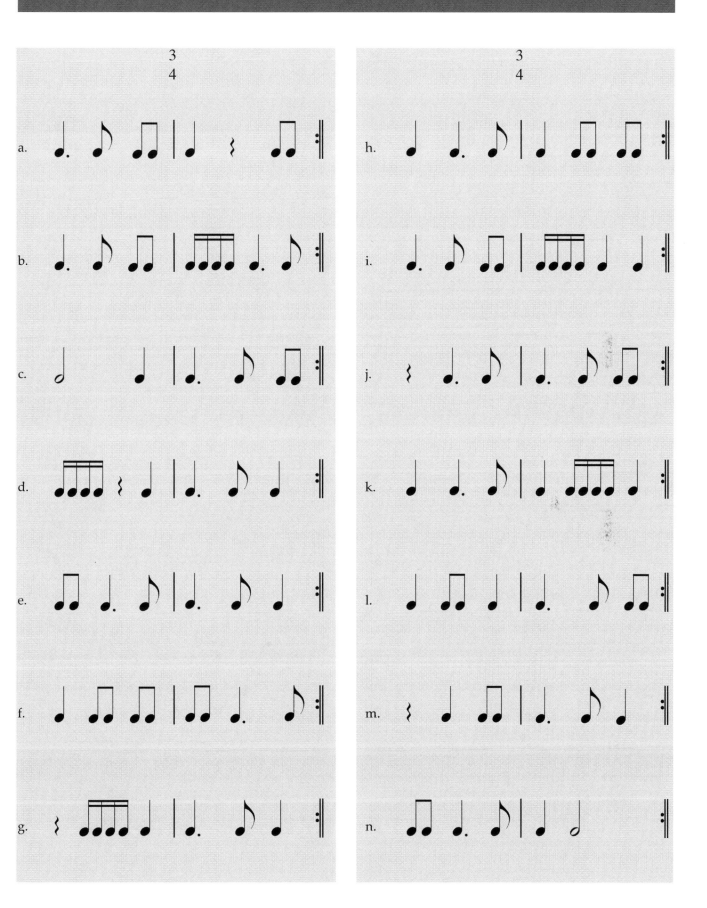

© 2018 Barbara M. Siemens PW-R2J

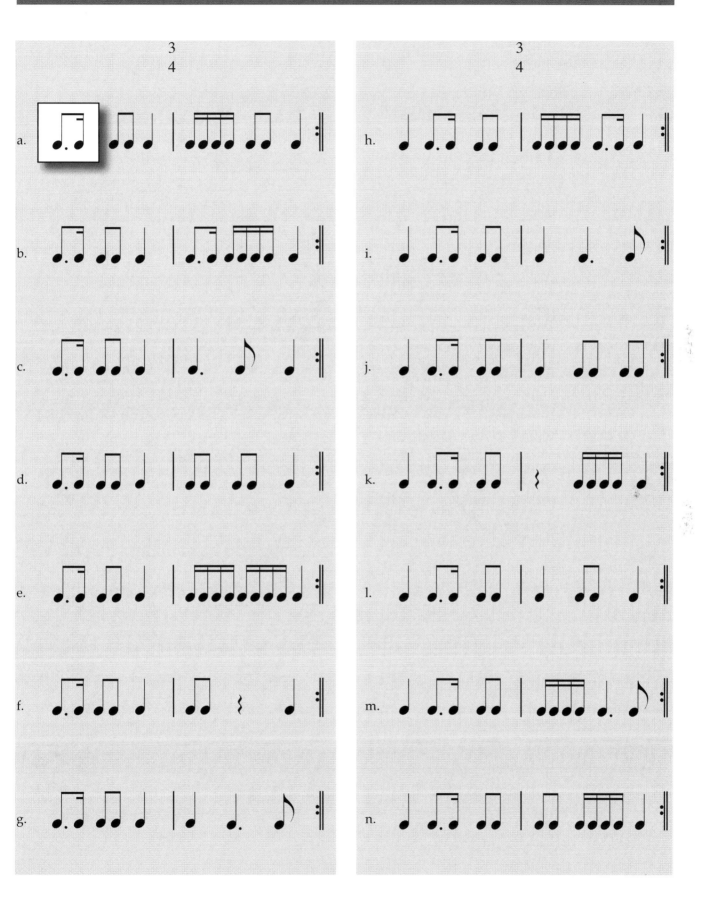

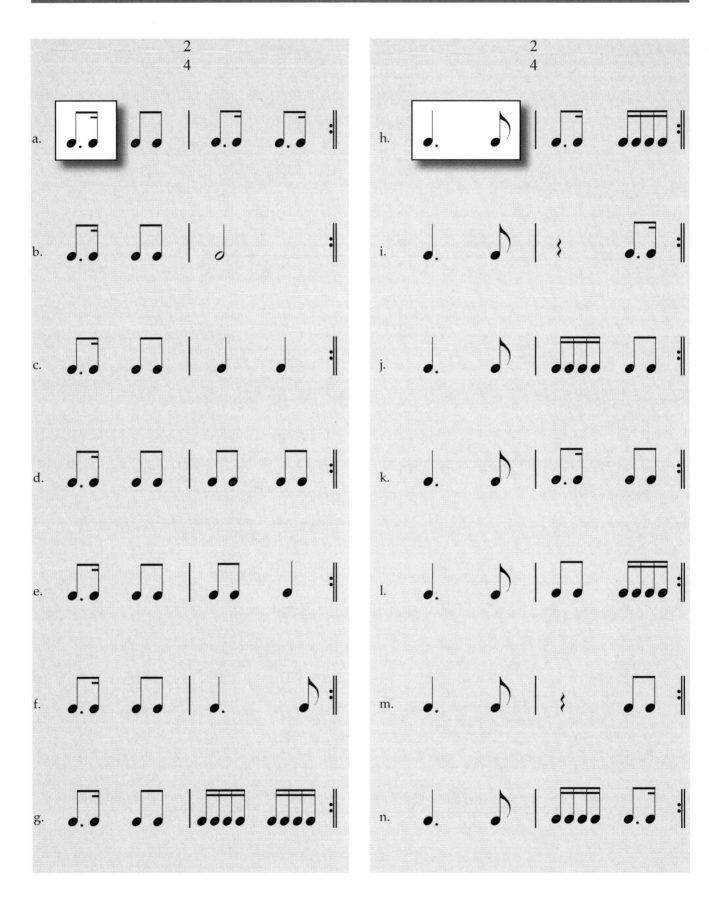

© 2018 Barbara M. Siemens PW-R2J

Junior

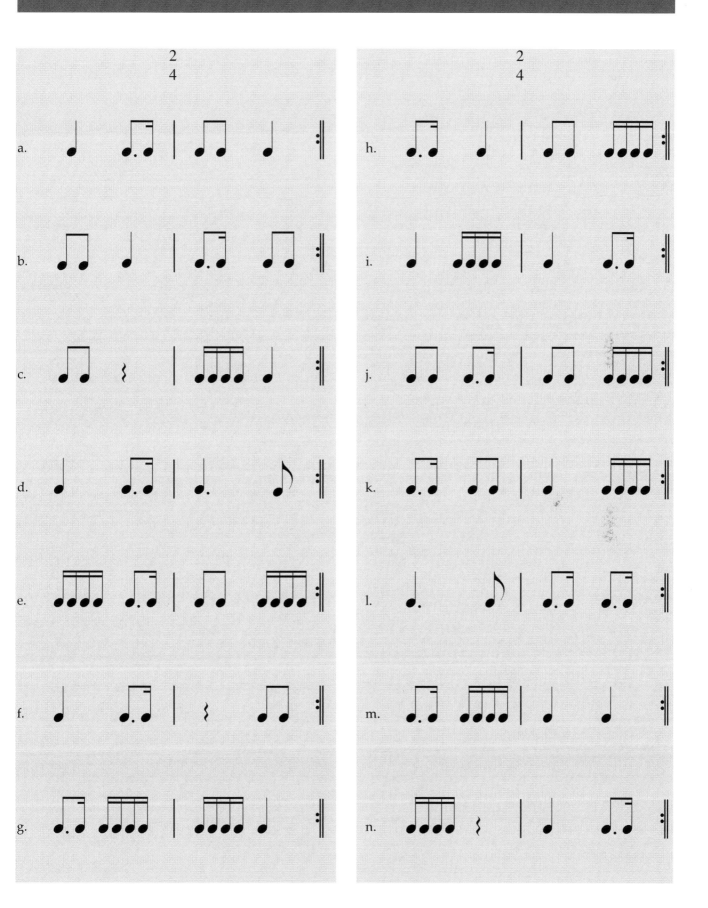

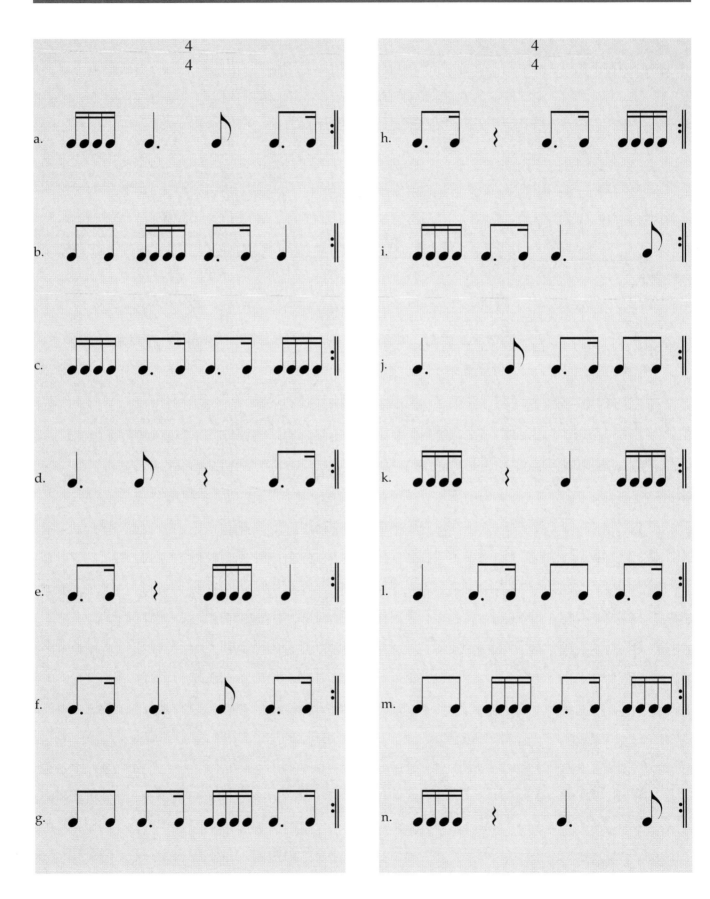

© 2018 Barbara M. Siemens   PW-R2J

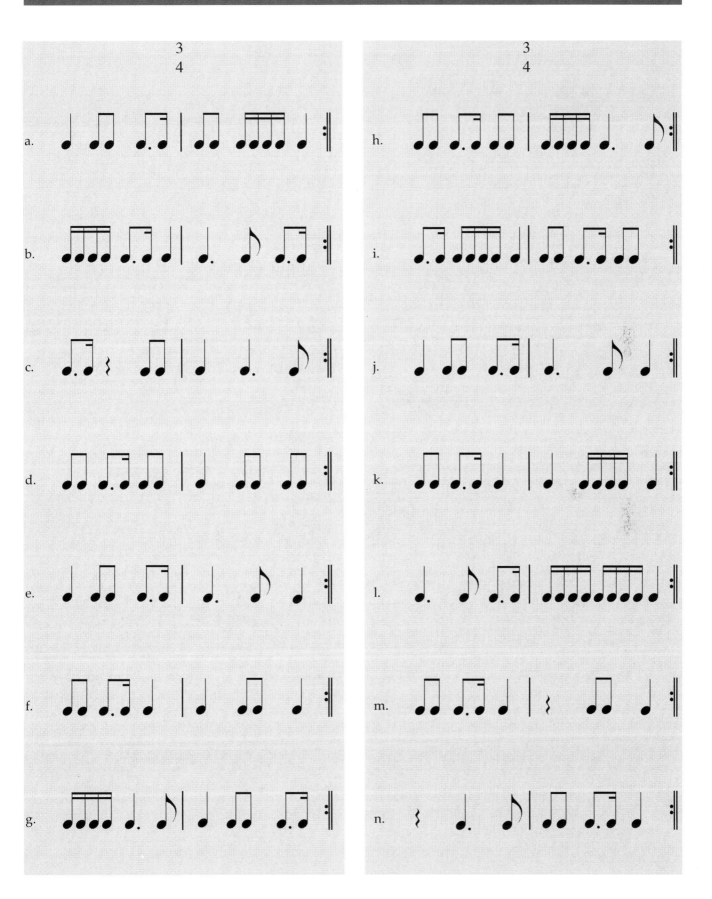

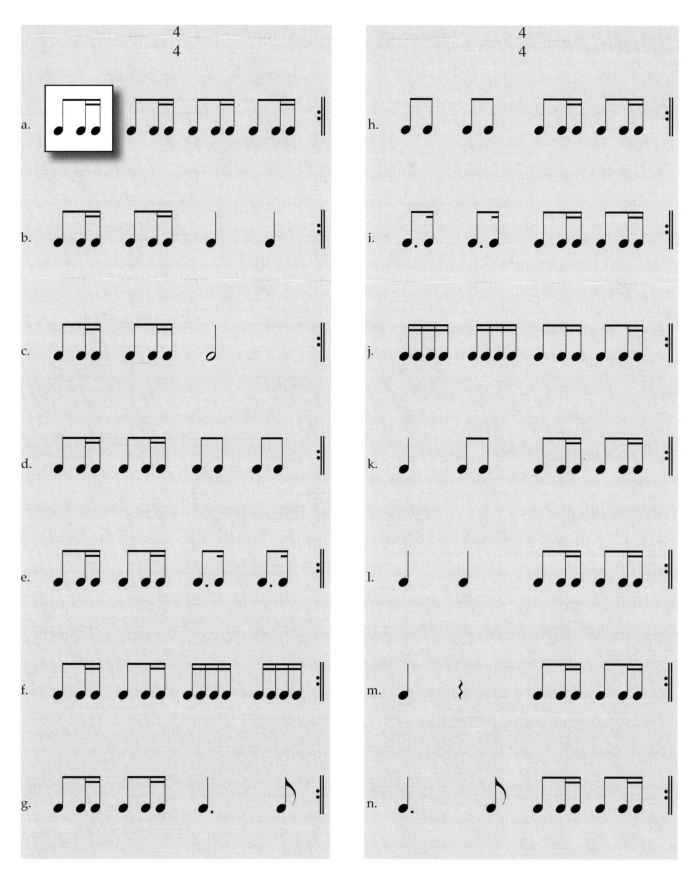

© 2018 Barbara M. Siemens PW-R2J

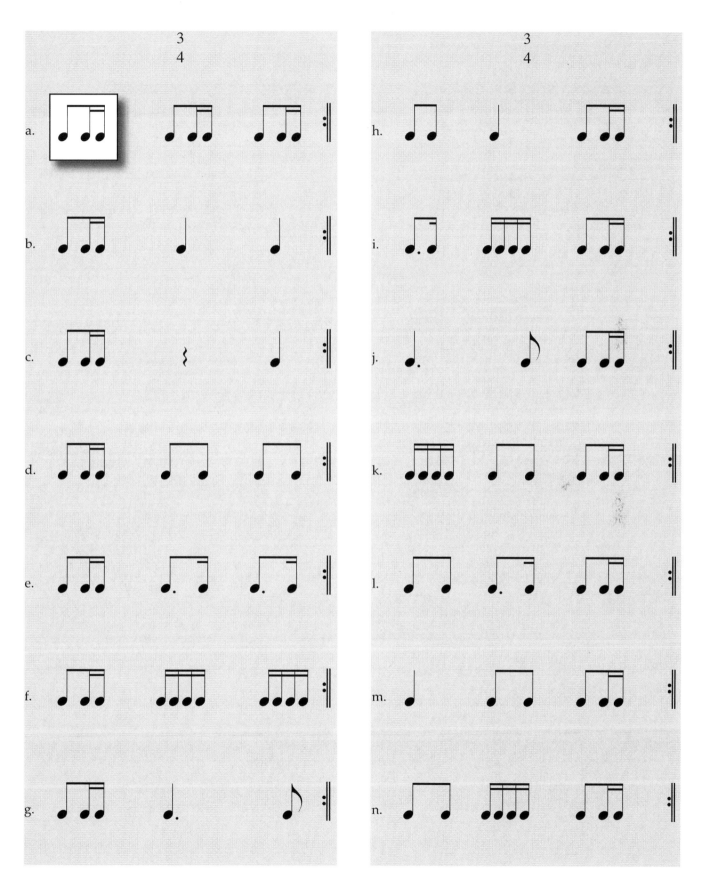

© 2018 Barbara M. Siemens   PW-R2J

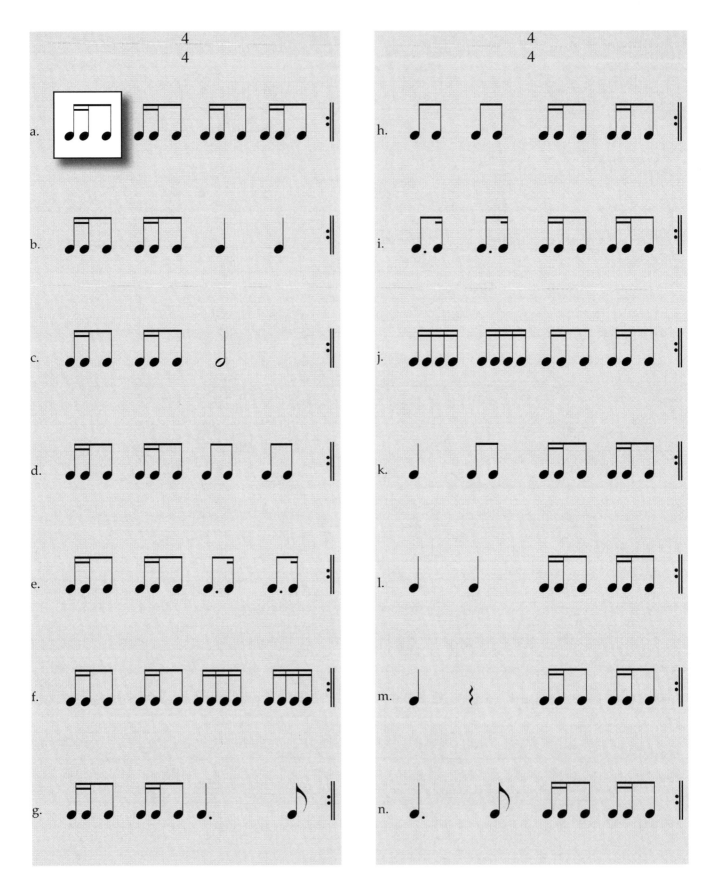

© 2018 Barbara M. Siemens PW-R2J

Junior

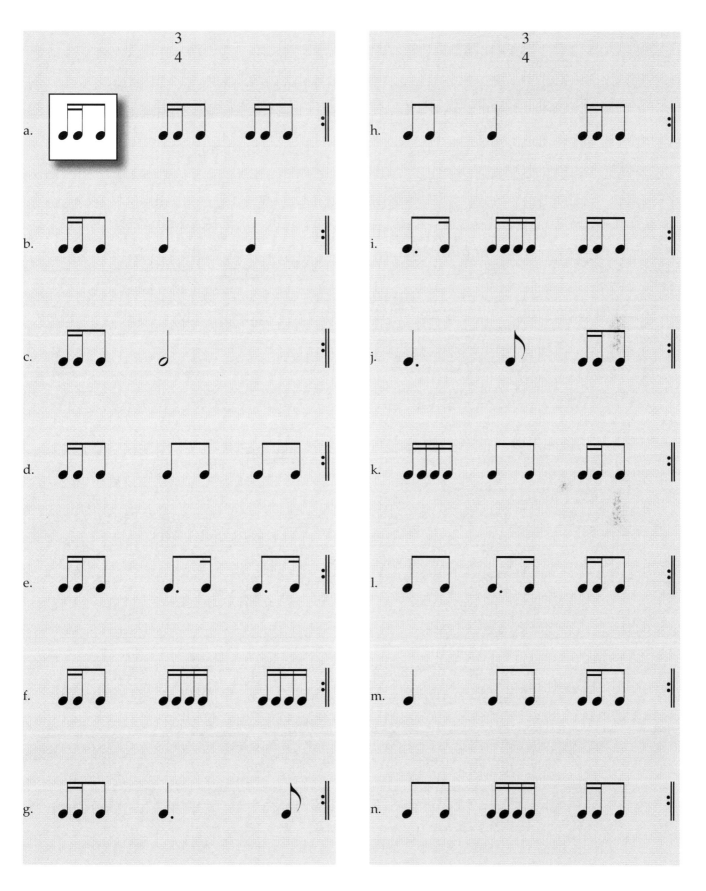

Junior

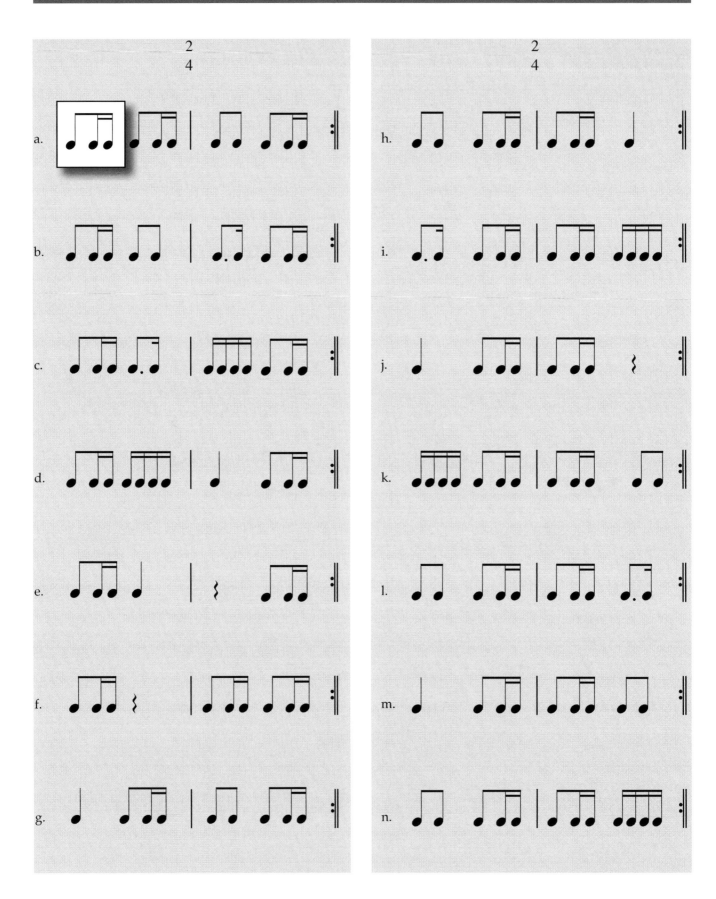

© 2018 Barbara M. Siemens   PW-R2J

Junior

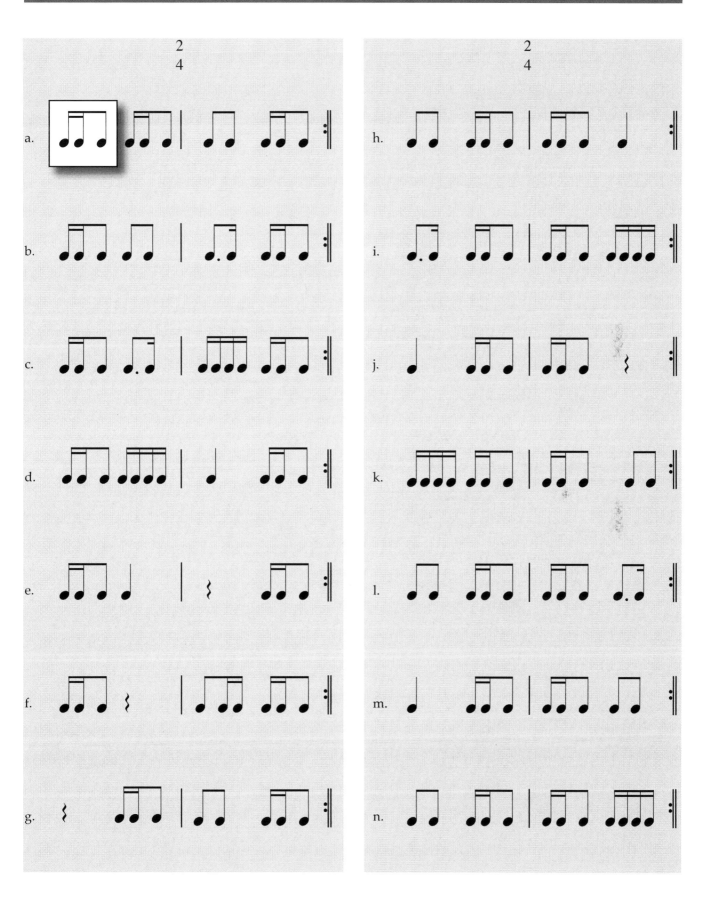

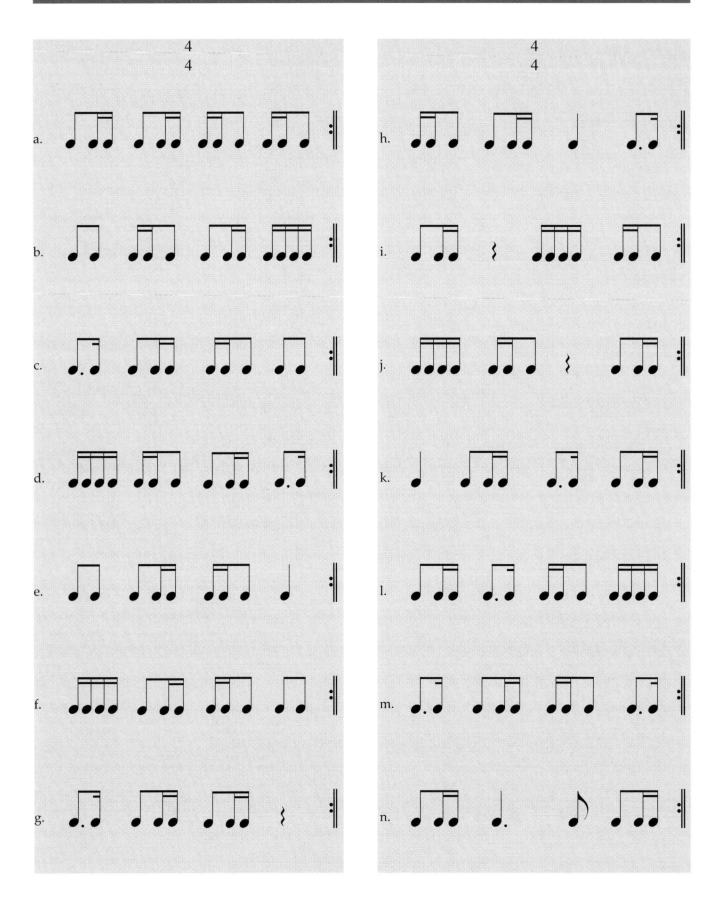

Junior

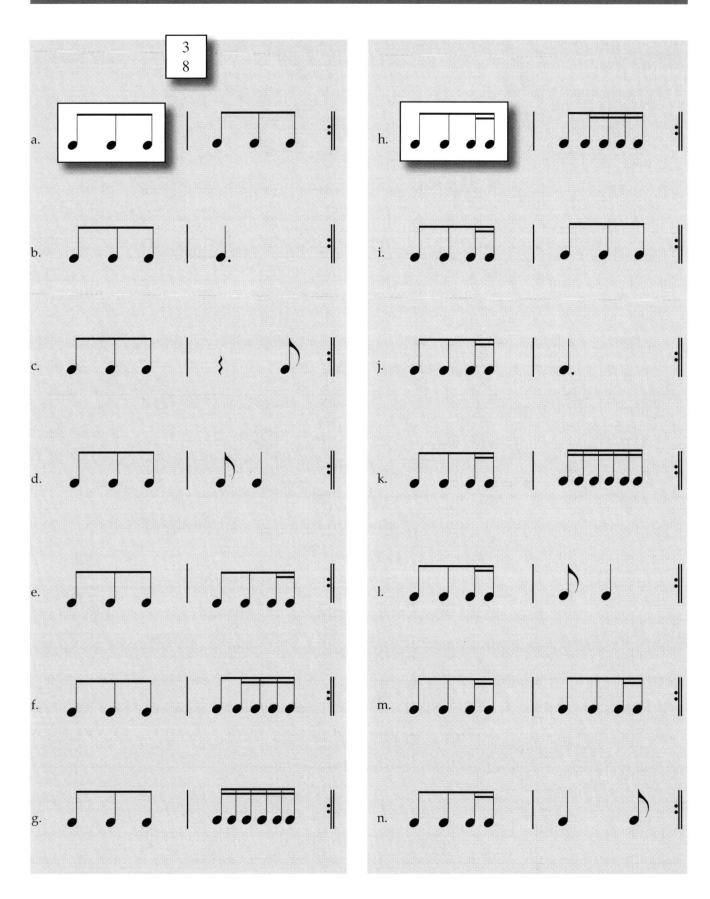

© 2018 Barbara M. Siemens   PW-R2J

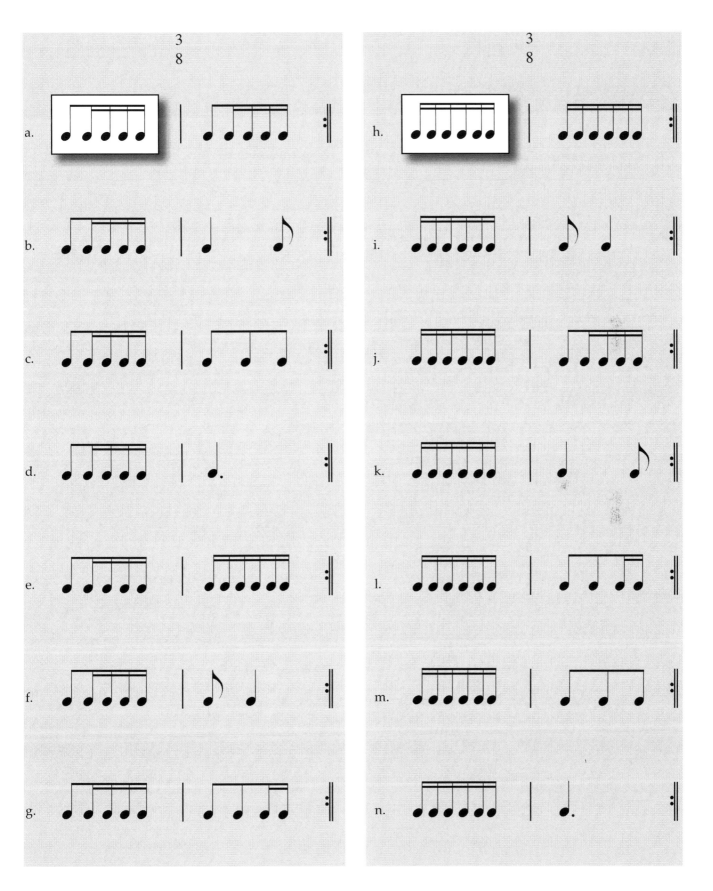

Junior

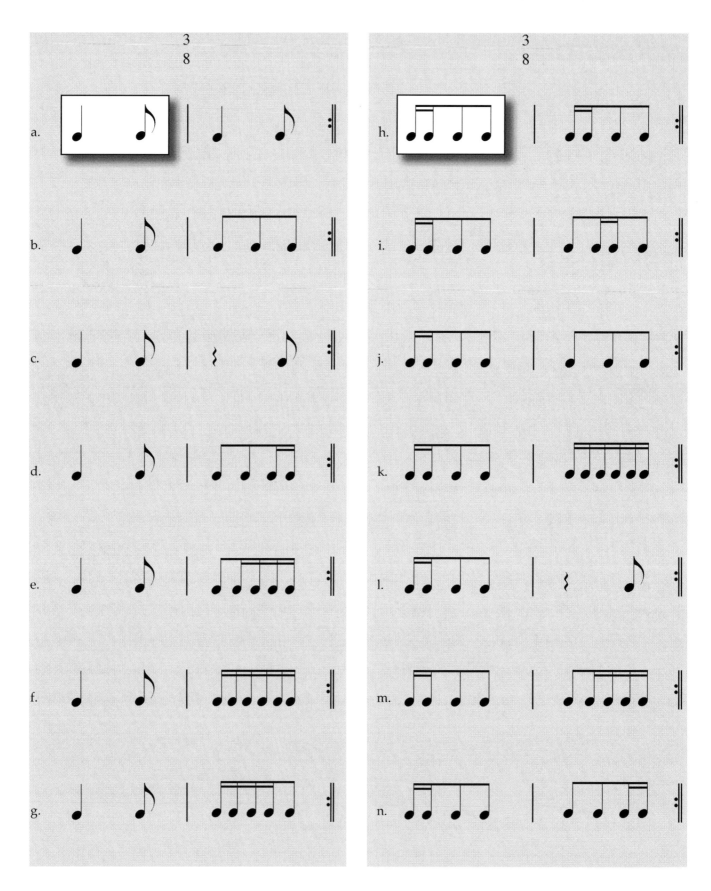

© 2018 Barbara M. Siemens PW-R2J

Junior

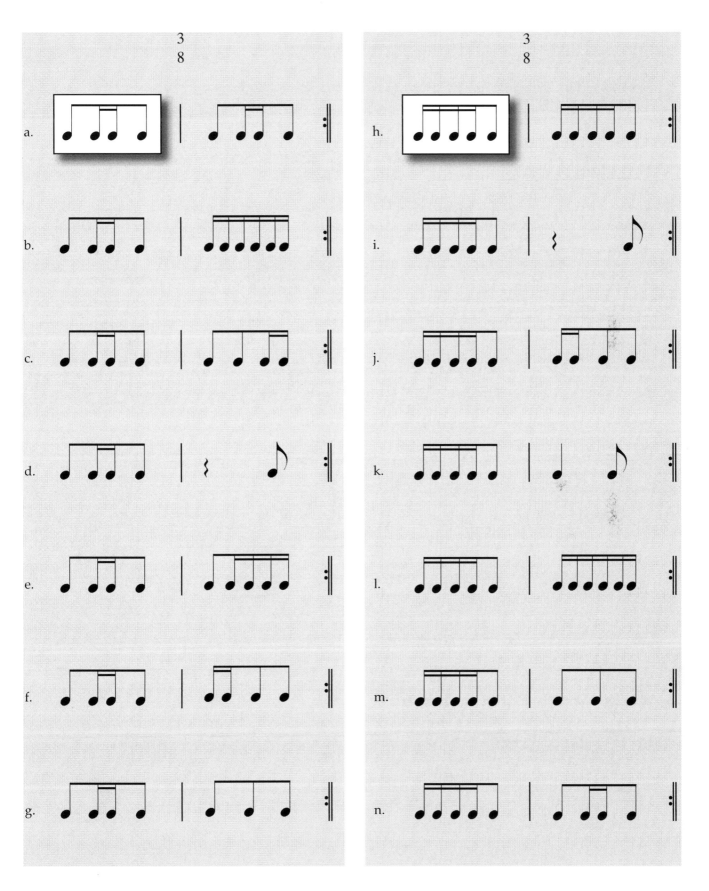

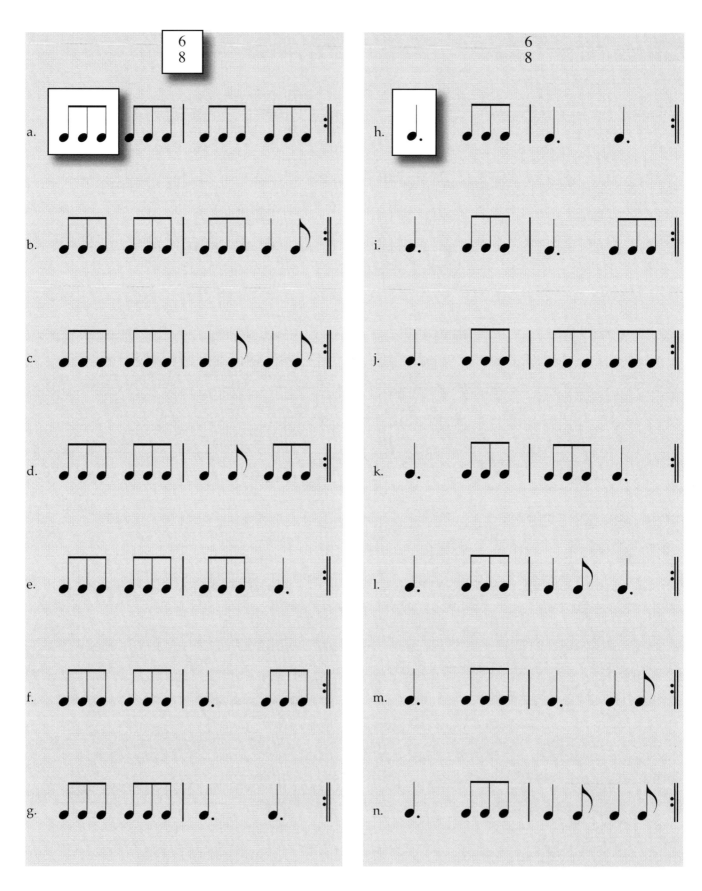

© 2018 Barbara M. Siemens PW-R2J

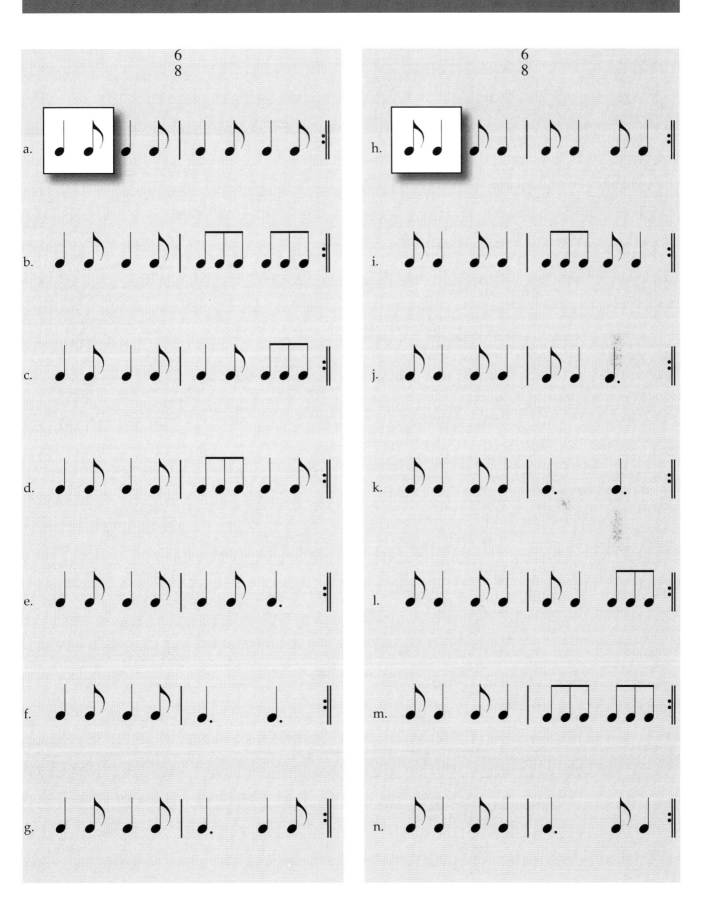

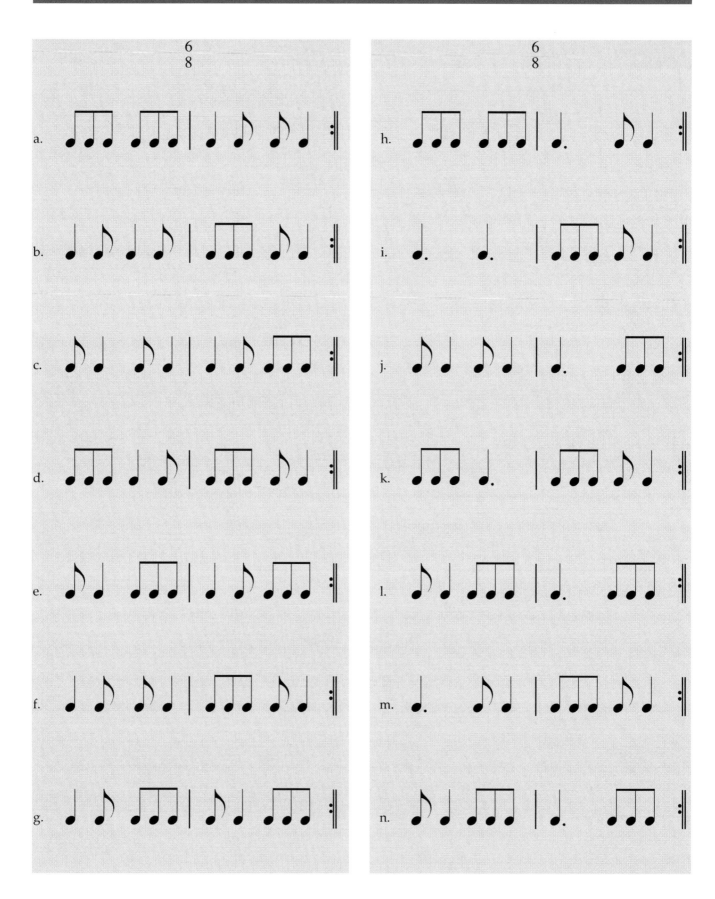

© 2018 Barbara M. Siemens   PW-R2J

Junior

© 2018 Barbara M. Siemens PW-R2J

Junior

5/4 (3 + 2)

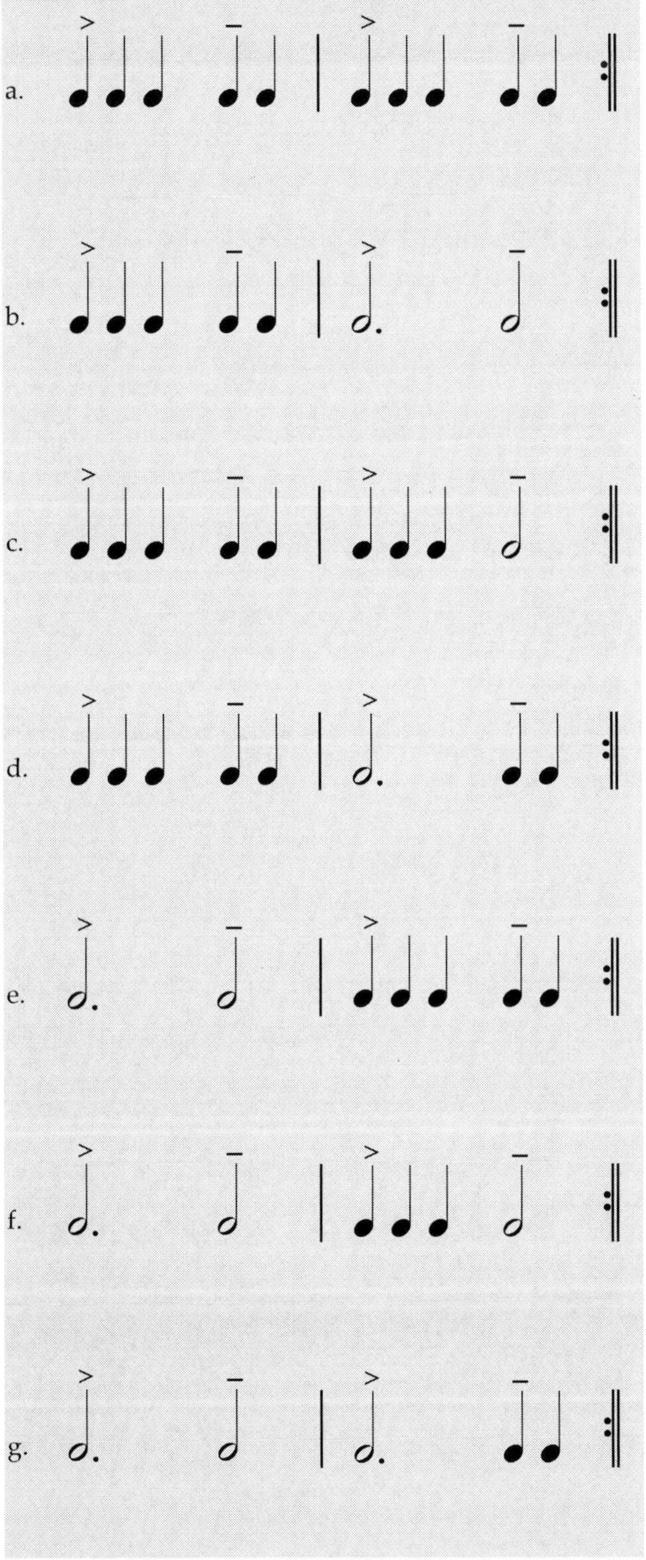

5/4 (2 + 3)

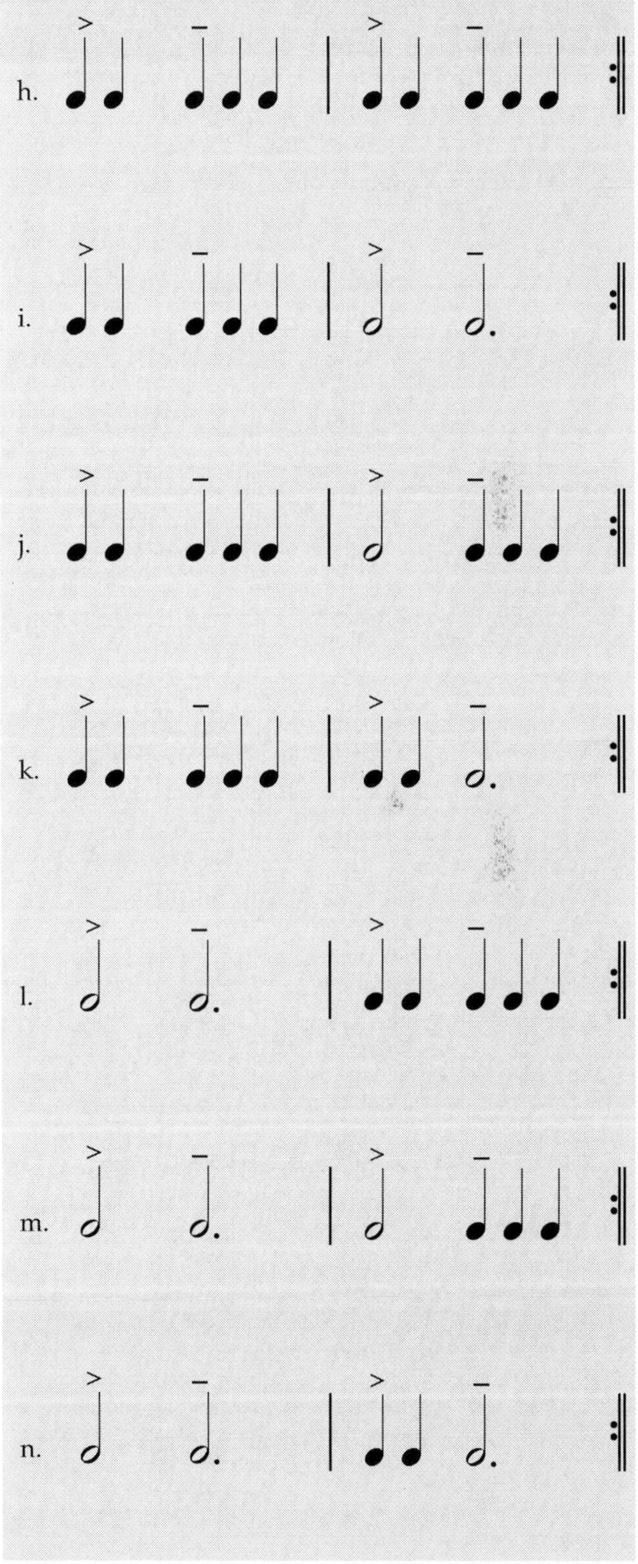

© 2018 Barbara M. Siemens PW-R2J

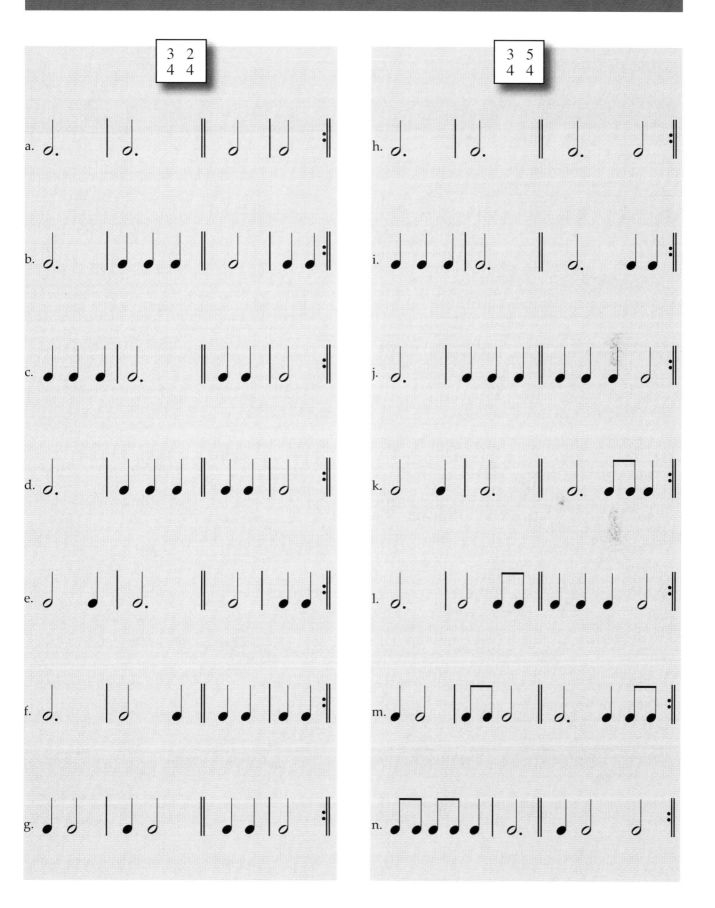

Junior

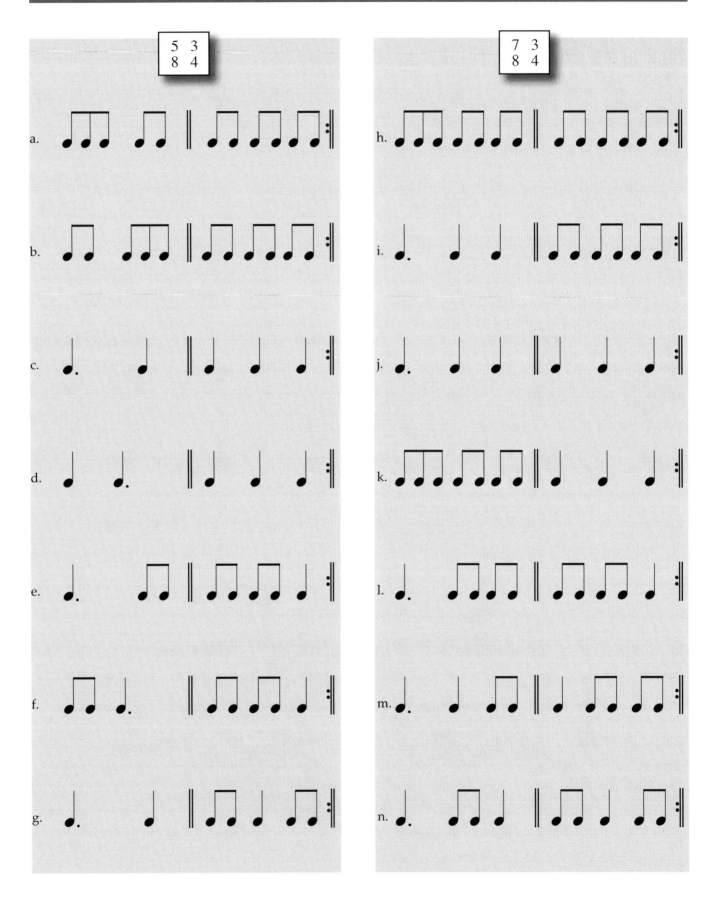

© 2018 Barbara M. Siemens PW-R2J

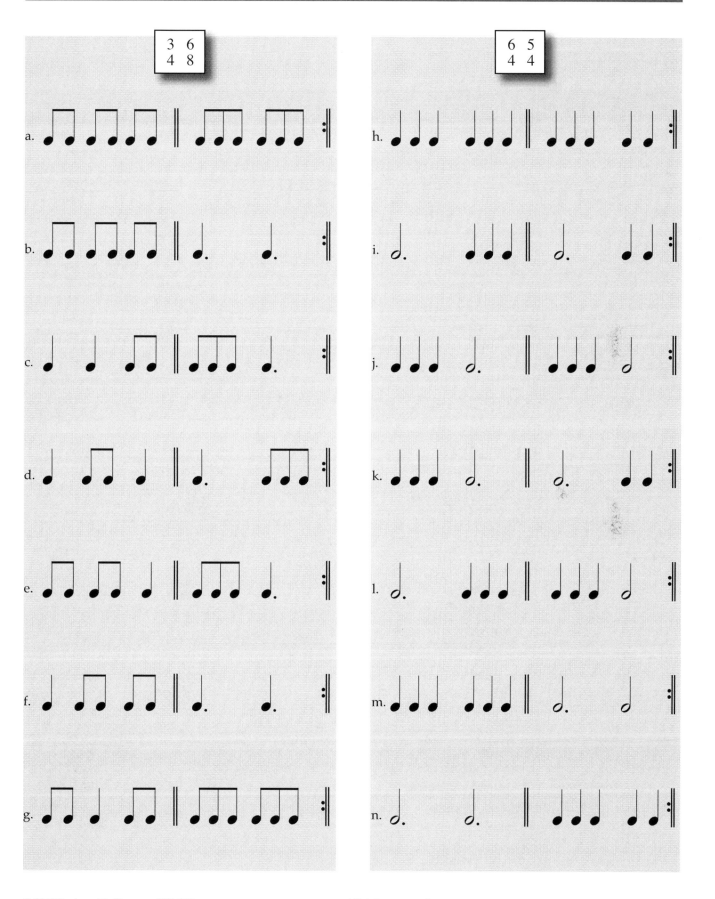

a.

b.

c.

d.

e.

f.

g.

h.

i.

j.

k.

l.

m.

n.

© 2018 Barbara M. Siemens   PW-R2J

a.

b.

c.

d.

e.

f.

g.

h.

i.

j.

k.

l.

m.

n.

a.

b.

c.

d.

e.

f.

g.

h.

i.

j.

k.

l.

m.

n.

© 2018 Barbara M. Siemens   PW-R2J

a.

b.

c.

d.

e.

f.

g.

h.

i.

j.

k.

l.

m.

n.

© 2018 Barbara M. Siemens   PW-R2J

Made in the USA
Columbia, SC
30 March 2022

58309771R00035